I0849892

nderstand the goodness of her

to know the warmth in a gra

lone, the good example she

ch she means from day to da

d things that children love.

e for her keeps growing too,

randmother's love has mean

ther love, how wise they d

ng hand, for children can

PRESENTED TO

_____

FROM

_____

DATE

Poems for Grandmother

A TAPESTRY OF LOVE

ART BY
GLENDA PUHEK

IDEALS PUBLICATIONS, A DIVISION OF GUIDEPOSTS
NASHVILLE, TENNESSEE

ISBN 0-8249-4111-X

Caseside printed in the U.S.A.
Text printed and bound in Mexico.
Printed by R.R. Donnelley & Sons.

Published by Ideals Publications, a division of Guideposts
535 Metroplex Drive, Suite 250
Nashville, Tennessee 37211
www.idealspublications.com

Library of Congress Cataloging-in-Publication Data
Poems for grandmother / [selected by Elizabeth Bonner Kea]; watercolors by
Glenda Puhek.
    p. cm.
    ISBN 0-8249-4111-X
    1. Grandmothers—Poetry. 2. American poetry. I. Kea, Elizabeth Bonner, 1976–
    PS595.G73 P59 2000
811.008′03520432—dc21   00-047221

10 8 6 4 2 1 3 5 7 9

POEMS SELECTED BY ELIZABETH BONNER KEA
DESIGNED BY EVE DeGRIE

ACKNOWLEDGMENTS

All possible care has been taken to fully acknowledge the ownership and use of every selection in this book. If any mistakes or omissions have occurred, they will be corrected in subsequent editions, provided notification is sent to the publisher. CROWELL, GRACE NOLL. "Old Mothers" from *Flame in the Wind.* Copyright © 1930, 1934 by Harper & Brothers. Copyright renewed 1952 by Grace Noll Crowell. Reprinted by permission of HarperCollins Publishers, Inc. HUFF, BARBARA. "Afternoon with Grandmother." Reprinted by permission of the author. JAQUES, EDNA. "A Child Needs a Grandma," "Garden Magic," and "My Grandma's Garden." Copyright © in Canada by Thomas Allen & Son Limited. Reprinted with permission. MURTON, JESSIE WILMORE. "Grandma's House" from *Whatsoever Things are Lovely.* Copyright © 1948 by Review and Herald Publishing Association. Used by permission. "Grandma's Kitchen" from *The Shining Thread.* Copyright © 1950 by the Pacific Press Publishing Association. Reprinted by permission of Pacific Press Publishing Association, Inc., Nampa, ID. Our sincere thanks to the following authors whom we were unable to locate: May Allread Baker for "To My Grandmother," Anne Campbell for "Grandmother's Rocker" and "A Memory," Meredith Gray for "Grandmother's Home," Reginald Holmes for "What Is a Grandmother?" and Mildred Maralyn Mercer for "A Tribute to Grandmother."

CONTENTS

GRANDMOTHER
IS . . .

My Song

I sing of you because your long
And busy days are gladly spent
In loving tasks, while your content
Spreads through our home like joyful song.

You quiet fear with tenderness;
Your laughter breaks the twilight gloom
Until sleep fills a moonlit room
And beholds the peace of Your caress.

Oh, gratefully my glad heart sings
A song of simple, happy days—
A grandmother's understanding ways,
And love that lives in little things.

—Ramona Vernon

OLD MOTHERS

They draw me to them: women who have grown
Wise with the wisdom that right living brings.
Old mothers who have suffered and have known
A triumph over many conquered things,
Who have grown gentle, trusting day by day,
Who have grown patient, serving through the years;
Who, having prayed much, have learned how to pray,
And weeping—learned how futile were their tears.

They wear such certainty within their eyes:
A sureness that no questioning can shake;
All is so clear to them—they are so wise,
The way was made so plain that they should take.
If one should come to them—his faith grown dim—
Their faith would light the fires anew in him.

—GRACE NOLL CROWELL

FOR SUCH AS YOU

For such as you, I do believe,
Spirits their softest carpets weave,
And spread them out with gracious hand
Wherever you walk, wherever you stand.

For such as you, of scent and dew
Spirits their rarest nectar brew,
And where you sit and where you sup
Pour beauty's elixir in your cup.

For all day long, like other folk,
You bear the burden, wear the yoke,
And yet when I look into your eyes at eve
You are lovelier than ever, I do believe.

—HERMANN HAGEDORN

YESTERDAY'S MOTHER

With courage and faith,
Tenderness and love,
She met the hardships
Of everyday life.

Ever envisioning for her children
A future bright with hope and success,
She was a daily example of her belief
That work shapes a day,
Days shape a life,
And character is the essence
Of all one's days—

A pioneer mother
Making a priceless contribution
To the ages.
—BERNICE C. HEISLER

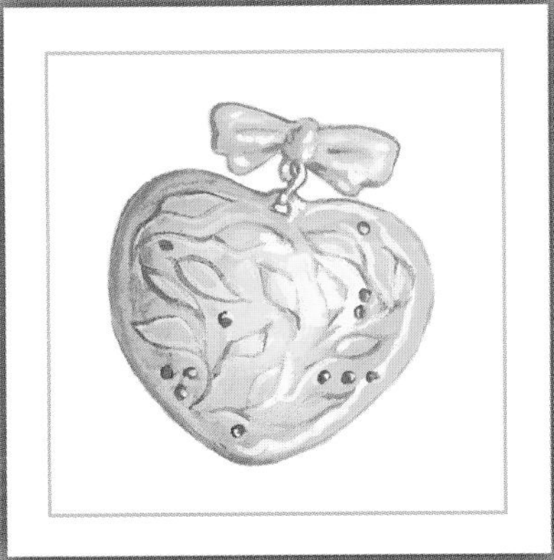

SOMEWHERE

Somewhere in the past
lie the roots to
a legacy of love,
of faith and hope
handed down through generations
of mothers.

Somewhere in the present
of everyday life
the thread continues,

POEMS FOR GRANDMOTHER

weaving imperceptibly
the bonds that stretch forth,
reaching

Somewhere into the future
where the legacy grows,
keeping alive the mothers
who have gone before
for all the children
who are to come.
—MARIANNE MILLER

GRANDMOTHER IS . . .

CHILDREN DO NOT REALIZE

Children do not realize
How deep is grandmother love, how wise —
They do not fully understand
The goodness of her guiding hand;
For children cannot even start
To know the warmth in Grandmother's heart,
The things she's done for them alone,
The good example she has shown.

And so they may not always say
How much she means from day to day,
And yet she's always held above
The childhood things that children love.
And as they grow the long years through
That love for her keeps growing too,
Until they learn the full extent
Of what a grandmother's love has meant.
—AUTHOR UNKNOWN

To know the warmth in a

alone, the good example sh

much she means from day to

hood thing... dren lo

ove for... owing

a grandm... has me

mother love, how wise they

...ding hand, for children ca

LOVE

Your love is like an island
In life's ocean, vast and wide;
A peaceful, quiet shelter
From the wind and rain and tide.

Above it, like a beacon light,
Shine faith and truth and prayer,
And through the changing scenes of life,
I find a haven there.

—AUTHOR UNKNOWN

GRANDMOTHER

They were lovely, all the grandmothers
Of the days of long ago,
With their gentle quiet faces
And their hair as white as snow.

They were growing old at fifty,
And at sixty donned lace caps,
At seventy clung to shoulder shawls
And loved their little naps.

But I love the modern grandmother
Who can share in all our joys,
And who understands the problems
Of her growing girls and boys.

She may boast that she is older,
But her heart is twenty-three . . .
My glorious bright-eyed grandmother,
Who is keeping young with me.

—AUTHOR UNKNOWN

MY GRANDMOTHER

I know a dear old lady
Whose voice is soft and low.
Her face is like some picture,
A dream of long ago;
She is not great or famous
Nor known in realm of art,
But she is rich in treasure
Which guides a kindly heart.

Her life a living sermon
Of hope and gentle acts,
A test for human nature
That's found in living facts;

She's patient, pure, and happy
In these her twilight days;
Her lips are ever ready
To comfort or to praise.

Her soul's a gleam of sunshine,
A rainbow in life's showers;
Her presence is a garden
Of ever-blooming flowers
Which time can never wither,
For recollections rare
Shall bloom around her mem'ry
And twine love's garlands there.
—AUTHOR UNKNOWN

GRANDMOTHER'S TAPESTRY

Throughout the years you've made no claim
To artistry; yet clear and fine
You've fashioned with your patient hands
A tapestry of rare design.

'Twas not with riches that you wove,
But chose for threads of precious gold
A childish kiss, a baby's smile,
Brave songs and dreams to clasp and hold.

—VERA L. SETER

to know the warmth in a gr

alone, the good example she

ch she means from day to

od thing   hen love

e for   owing too

grandm   has mea

other love, how wise they

ing hand, for children can

WHAT IS A GRANDMOTHER?

She's younger than springtime,
With stars in her eyes
   Or a silver-haired angel
  In a mortal's disguise.
When you're feeling let down
And a shadow appears,
Just the touch of her hand
Will banish your fears.

She's a practical nurse
Who knows how to heal;
And when a crisis arrives,
She is stronger than steel.

When a family has problems,
As quick as you please
She straightens them out
With the greatest of ease.

She's adept at surprises
Or telling stories at night;
She's the cookie jar keeper
And a grandchild's delight.
She knows all the angles
And what life is about—
A grandmother is someone
We couldn't do without.
　　—REGINALD HOLMES

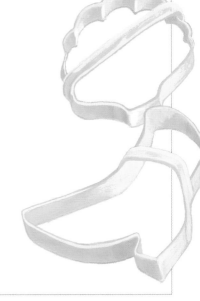

A Child Needs a Grandma

A child needs a grandma to spoil him a bit,
Someone with time on her hands who will sit
In an old-fashioned rocker that shivers and squeaks
And listen to words that a little boy speaks.

Someone who knows how a gingerbread man,
All crumbly and fragrant and warm from the pan,
Can comfort a fellow who feels a bit blue,
And nothing just right seems to happen to you.

A child needs a grandma to teach him the words
That run like a hymn in the song of the birds,
Someone who knows where the orioles go
When the garden is covered with inches of snow.

For only grandma remembers to say
"Now be a good boy" as she tucks him away
Under the covers and pats them down tight,
For little boys sometimes get scared in the night.

A child needs the comforting knowledge of love,
Steady and sure as the stars up above,
To carry him safely through sunshine and tears,
A light in the darkness, a stay through the years.

A child needs a grandma to nod in her chair
And give him her blessing by just being there.
—EDNA JAQUES

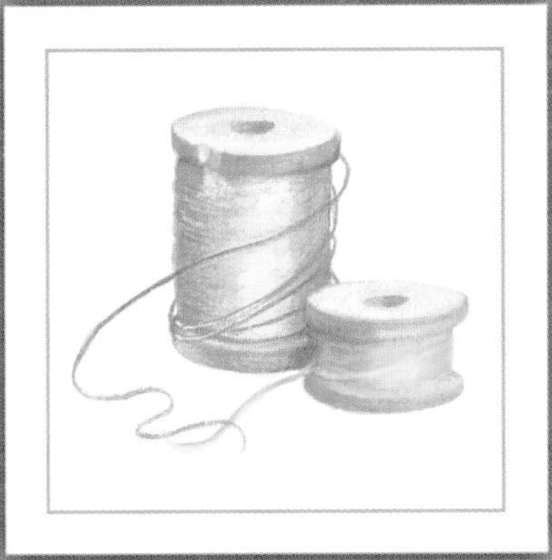

GUARDIAN

The moon is but a candleglow
That flickers thro' the gloom;
The starry space, a castle hall;
And Earth, the children's room,
Where all night long the old trees stand
To watch the streams asleep:
Grandmothers guarding trundle beds,
Good shepherds guarding sheep.

— VACHEL LINDSAY

AFTERNOON WITH GRANDMOTHER

I always shout when Grandma comes,
But Mother says, "Now please be still
And good and do what *Grandma* wants."

So off we go in Grandma's car.
"There's a brand new movie quite near by,"
She says, "that I'd rather like to see."
And I say, "So would I."

The show has horses and chases and battles;
We gasp and hold hands the whole way through.
She smiles and says, "I liked that lots."
And I say, "I did too."

"It's made me hungry, though," she says,
"I'd like a malt and tarts with jam.
By any chance are you hungry too?"
And I say, "Yes, I am."

Later at home my mother says,
"I hope you were careful to do as bid.
Did you and Grandma have a good time?"
And I say, "YES, WE DID!"
—BARBARA A. HUFF

GRANDMOTHER'S HOME

GRANDMOTHER'S HOME

I dream—
Of a friendly tree with boughs outstretched
To welcome me home when my heart needs rest;
Of a flower-lined walk, smiling gay and sweet,
That beckons my step and gladdens my feet;
Of an open door round whose worn sill twines
The secret of peace in wisteria vines—
And the blessed vision of your dear face,
Grandmother-mine—by the fireplace.

I turn from striving that seemed worthwhile,
To the sure serenity of your smile;
To your voice of love with enduring charms—
The end of the road is your sheltering arms.

—MEREDITH GRAY

GRANDMOTHER'S HOUSE

In Grandmother's house, when the morn creeps in
Through the heart of each windowpane,
I awake a king 'neath a patchwork quilt,
To the warmth of a loved domain.
Oh, never a house that can tuck you in
With such calm when the day is done.
Oh, never a house that holds out as much
When another day has begun.

When the chimney sighs with the autumn wind
And the sashes take up the beat,
The old oil lamp casts a soften glow
On a scene that is dear and sweet.
The firelight dances from the maple logs
To the book at Grandma's knee;
The grandfather clock stands almost hushed,
So upright and reverent is he.

Staunch, faithful and old, it stands there unmoved
Through the storms of the changing years;
It shelters the lost, the weary, the weak,
And never knows doubting or fears.

Oh, little old house, sun-mellowed and calm,
Reach out to me ever, I pray,
And gather me close, as close to your heart
As you do in this treasured day.

—S. BARLOW BIRD

GRANDMOTHER'S KITCHEN

Yes, it is ever so simple:
The rough-hewn floor, yet scrubbed so bright;
The huge shining range with a warming oven;
A teakettle steaming to the side;
And, pride of all, there is an old sink
With a hand pump to draw water,
So fresh, so cool, deep from the well.

Muslin curtains at the windows—
Starched stiff, like Sunday's petticoat:
A handmade, braided rug or two,
Covering the worn spots on the floor;
Geraniums on the windowsill;
Rosemary and marjoram too—

Not so much to dress the window,
But grown to flavor Grandma's stew.

An ancient rocker near the stove,
Giving the same comfort and solace
To tired hearts and minds
As the long forgotten cradling
Each man has known in Mother's arms;

A kitten or two romping and playing;
And a dog, on winter nights,
Allowed to stay close to the fire —
Where frost-nipped toes are often left
To rest upon the oven door
Till glowing warmth returns once more.

continued on next page

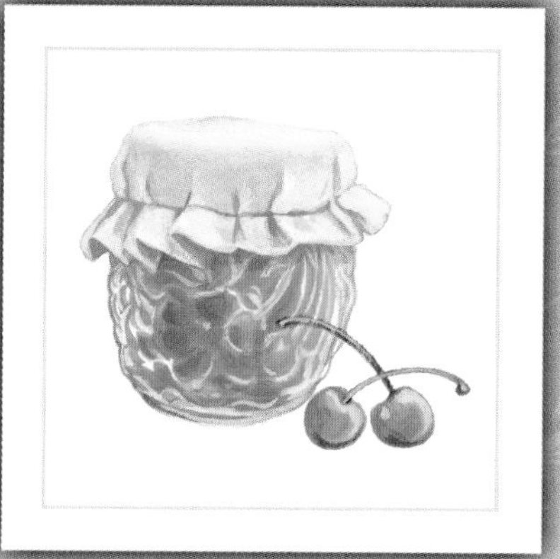

The pot of ever-brewing coffee —
Always ready to be poured,
To comfort hearts on chilly nights
With the warmth of friendship true.

Cupboard shelves filled on Saturday,
To last throughout the week — with hams,
And roasts and sausages, fresh-smoked;
Pies and cakes, and coffee kuchen;

Yes, it is ever simple;
But so is the heart.
—VIVIAN VOLK

KITCHEN REVERIE

In your big old-fashioned kitchen
In a river valley town,
I can hear you softly singing
In your rose sprigged gingham gown.

I can see your black stove gleaming
Above white scrubbed floors of pine
With your high scrim-curtained windows
Framed with ripe grapes on the vine.

I can smell the sweet aroma
Of jam bubbling in the pot
And the stack of golden flapjacks
Spread with sorghum, piping hot.

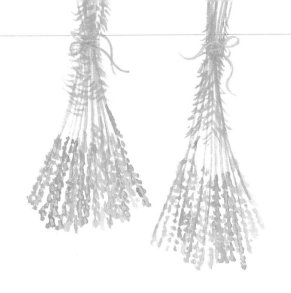

I can feel your love around me
In your smile and in your eyes,
Turning your cozy kitchen
Into a paradise.
— CATHERINE GRAYMAN

GRANDMOTHER'S HOME 43

GRANDMA'S KITCHEN

It was not Grandma's parlor that we loved—
A place for times when "company" was about—
Where children entered awed, and breathlessly,
And tiptoed noiselessly and gladly out.

I keep a shelf for tiny bowls and pans,
And always give small children bits of dough—
Remembering a warm and spicy smell,
A sunny kitchen—in the long ago.
—JESSIE WILMORE MURTON

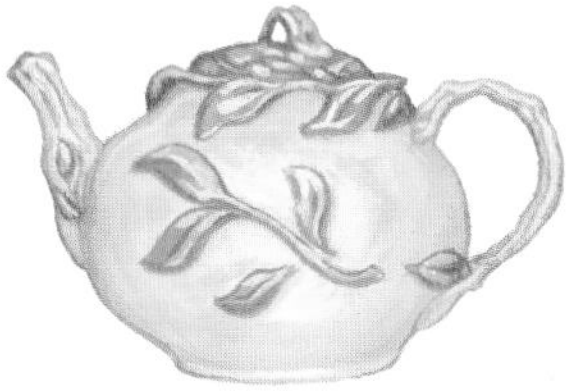

GRANDMA'S HOUSE

There's a house upon a hillside,
Seems it's stood for centuries there;
There's a footpath to the doorway
And a garden kept with care.

There's a kitchen filled with living
And sweet-smelling things there are,
Like apple pies a-baking
And a great big cookie jar.

Seems the kettle is always singing
And the place is bright and warm—
Gives the feeling of contentment
Like a shelter from the storm.

There's a chair that creaks when rocking
And a big cat fast asleep;
There's a grandfather clock-a-ticking
And a knitting basket heap.

There's a dear, sweet lady waiting,
For, you see, this is her house;
Yes, I'll always find a welcome
When I visit Grandma's house.
—WINNIFRED ELSAESSER

GRANDMOTHER'S
GARDEN

THE GARDEN

Grandmother's garden is lovely and calm:
    Savory lemon, and chive.

Grandmother's garden is close by a hill:
    Marjoram, basil, and balm.

Grandmother's garden has bees in a hive:
    Cardamom, curry, and dill.

Grandmother's garden has a fountain and chime:
    Sesame, fennel, and bay.

Grandmother's garden smells sweet in the dew.
    Lavender, lovage, and thyme.

Grandmother's garden — a vintage sachet —
    Rosemary, anise, and rue.

—EDNA OWENS ERGEN

Reverie

So beautiful in my grandmother's garden
Deep in velvet shadow
Where the lilies of the valley grow.
Aware of flower fragrance and earth fragrance
Of cool and wet and early
And the earth springing back behind the footfall.
Picking the lilies of the valley,
Dew in flower cups

While the first carriage clatters
Over the cobblestones on High Street
And the church bells are calling, calling, calling
From the open kitchen window
Down the dawning summer morning
Through the clamor and clatter
And the clip-clop of hoofbeats
And the fragrance.

—DOROTHY HERRING

My Grandma's Garden

The flowers of my grandma's day
Were just as fragrant, just as gay;
The bleeding hearts, the larkspur blue,
Did something to the heart of you,
And printed deep on memory's page
The blueprint of your heritage.

A climbing rose that used to peep
Into her room to watch her sleep,
Hollyhocks yellow as the sun
That grew beside the chicken run,
    Snapdragons on a stately stem,
     And candy tuft to nod at them.

    A snowball tree by the front door
Sprinkled its petals on the floor,

While ragged robins used to vie
With phlox to charm the passerby,
And once a bush of juniper
Broke into lovely bloom for her.

But sweeter than a Sultan's crown
Was Grandma in her lilac gown,
Walking among her flowers, knowing
That lavender and rue were growing.
And somehow her old kindly face
Was part and parcel of the place,
Giving it dignity and pride
As if a light were on inside.
— EDNA JACQUES

To My Grandmother

In childhood days, dear Grandmother, it was you
Who taught me all of nature's loveliness.
How, from sodden leaf mold, violets grew
To fragrant beauty 'neath the sun's caress.
You pointed out the tender, living green
Of lichen growing on the rocky ledge;
The mullein stalk, like plush; the mellow sheen
Of bittersweet, twined on the frosted hedge.
You taught the gracefulness of leafless trees
(Their twigs wove tapestry against the sky),
And in the thaw-wet furrows, even these
Would bear the gold of harvest by and by.

And I in wood, in field, in bare brown sod,
Found everywhere the hidden touch of God.

—MAY ALLREAD BAKER

To Grandmother — My Garden

Your heart, it always seems to me,
Is like a garden fair:
A blending of beautiful colors,
Sweet fragrance everywhere.

Pansies, of course, are
Your thoughtfulness;
Red roses, your love so deep;
Dark purple iris, your sympathy
To smooth roads rough and steep.

Violets and forget-me-nots,
Nestling close to Old Mother Earth,
Mean your ever-wise understanding
For healing the world's little hurts.

Vines, with their clinging fingers,
Are your loving arms so strong;
The green of their leafy verdure,
Your faith in me, right or wrong.

Everything in my garden,
Caressed by God's sunshine and dew,
Tells of the love undying,
Deep in the heart of you.
—LOLA TAYLOR HEMPHILL

GARDEN MAGIC

She has the gift of growing things,
A magic touch with plant and flower;
The frailest slips will grow for her,
Touched by her finger's tender power.
We ask her how she makes them grow,
She laughs and says she loves them so.

Her windowsills are always gay,
With blooms of every shade and hue;
She's always setting out new bulbs,
You know, the way some women do.
She digs around the soil and sands,
Putting it down with loving hands.

And sometimes just when twilight creeps
Across the gardens of the town,
I see her walking lovingly
Amongst her flowers up and down.
Her garments glowing in the night,
As if she walks in paths of light.

I do not think life could bestow
A finer gift than loving toil:
The joy of helping things to grow,
Of working with the sun and soil,
That every soul you meet and know
Is lovelier because of you.

—EDNA JAQUES

OLD-FASHIONED FLOWERS

I like old-fashioned flowers,
The kind that Grandma grows,
Like tidy bachelor buttons
Of white and blue and rose;
Like friendly pansy faces
As golden as the sun,
Trimmed in purple like the sky
We see when day is done;
Like stiffly petaled zinnias
As bright as flowers can be,

Like tall and stately hollyhocks,
The rainbow hued sweetpea;
Like morning glories climbing up,
In bright blue, tangled rows—
I love old-fashioned flowers,
The kind that Grandma grows.

—VIRGINIA BLANCK MOORE

MEMORIES
SHARED

Two Grandmothers

They talk of life as they had lived it when,
Some sixty years ago, they both were young;
Bright little memories, like golden beads
Upon the frailest silver necklace strung.

Each memory revives some incident
Of early married life, of hardships shared,
Of children gathered round, of work and play,
Of little broken hopes by love repaired.

I see the picture which they paint; brushed
With shaky hands upon time's canvas, spread
For two grandmothers who are busily,
With shining shuttle, weaving memories' thread.

— INGA GILSON CALDWELL

Grandmother's Thoughts

Grandmother dear, as you sit in your chair,
Of what do you think when you smile?
I have often watched when you knew it not,
And guessed at your thoughts for awhile.

Do you think of the days in the long ago —
Of things too sweet to confide;
Tender memories of your girlhood days
That still in your heart abide?

Do you dream of babies tucked in to sleep,
Of lullabies sung soft and low?
Grandmother dear, those stories you told
Are the ones I love best, you know.

Dream on, smile on, my grandmother dear,
Of things you have long loved best;
Though it isn't meant for me to know
About the treasured thoughts in your breast.
—MARTHA JUNE MOAD

A Memory

When I am old, and dreaming by the fire,
One memory I'll keep until the close.
A little yard where honeysuckle grows,
A house whose walls surround my heart's desire.

A porch, well-guarded by twin maple trees,
A lighted window and an old armchair,
A row of books, a gently sloping stair,
The scent of roses on the summer breeze.

One memory I'll keep and never tire,
A little house, a friendly maple tree,
And by the open fire, your smile for me—
When I am old, and dreaming by the fire.
—ANNE CAMPBELL

My Grandmother

She has about her the quality
Of a summer willow —
A pleasantness that seems to say,
"Come, sit in my shade
And look at the quiet goodness of earth."

She has within her a constancy
Which never blares or barbs,
But speaks to one who listens
Of His love.

Somehow in her truth
The storm of life becomes the kiss of raindrops.

—SHIRLEY GARFIN

FOR MY GRANDMA

Because you rocked my father
To sleep when he was small,
And hastened to his crib-side
Whenever you heard him call,
Because you told him stories
And fed him bread and jam
And baked his birthday cakes
And pushed him in his pram,

Because you kissed his tears away
And prayed for him each night
And in your kind and gentle way
Taught him to do the right:
Because I love him, just as you,
And because I too now have a son,
You are often in my prayers,
When the weary day is done.
— MARY ELLEN STELLING

GRANDMOTHER'S ROCKER

She is cuddling the baby in Grandmother's rocker,
And singing an old-time song;
In this armchair my grandmother once rocked Mother,
Her arms, like her love, were strong;
And the dear little baby she used to hold
Is a woman now, with the long years told.

There is something enchanting about that old rocker;
So easy it is to sway
With an infant to guide on the road to slumber,
To dreams of a bygone day,
And the time when a baby knew all life's charms
In the loving curve of her mother's arms.

She is singing to baby in Grandmother's rocker,
The cycle of life goes on.
For many a baby from Grandmother's rocker
Is out in the world and gone;
And the kindly creak of the rocking chair
Is the echo of more than one woman's prayer.

—ANNE CAMPBELL

Twilight Stories

Neither daylight, starlight, moonlight,
But a sad-sweet term of some light
By the saintly name of twilight.

The Grandma twilight stories!—Still
A childish listener, I hear
The katydid and whipporwill,
In deepening atmosphere

Of velvet dusk, blent with the low
Soft music of the voice that sings
And tells me tales of long ago
And old enchanted things. . . .

While far fails the last dim daylight,
And the fireflies in the twilight
Drift about like flakes of starlight.
—JAMES WHITCOMB RILEY

To Grandma

I remember you in my growing-up years,
When you kissed my hurts and soothed my fears.
The world seemed such a foreboding place
Till I saw its beauty upon your face.

Those years are gone, but the feeling's still there,
Rooted in the memories we share:
Memories of endless walks on the beach
When your gentle wisdom was within my reach;
Of baking bread and holding hands
And bedtime stories of distant lands.

And although we never spoke out loud,
Those words that humble the stubborn and proud,
Somehow I think we always knew
That you love me as I love you.

—KAREN H. DUSEK

GRANDMA'S HOUSE

My grandma's house was wide and white,
With flagstones winding to the door;
And there was laughter there,
And playthings on the floor.

The orchard was a storyland
For children, with its gnarled old trees—
In autumn, gay with glowing fruit,
In spring, with bloom and bees.

And how we loved the gray springhouse
Of mossy stones and sparkling stream,
With rows of yellow butter pats
And crocks of thick, sweet cream.

There are so many things about
My childhood I cannot recall;
But of my grandma's house, it seems
That I remember all.
—JESSIE WILMORE MURTON

MEMORIES AT GRANDMOTHER'S

Grandmother's house had a long, wide piazza,
A hammock, a cup for Grandpa's mustache,
A pump that squeaked—and I had a white dress
Circled about with a pink satin sash.

Grandmother's hat had ostrich plumes on it,
She wafted a fan in the family pew,
And I wore the white dress with a guimpe and a bonnet
And squeaky shoes that were shiny and new.

Summertime—lazily hammock was swinging,
Dolls in a cozy nook; on a sweet-scented night,
Fireflies glimmered, a whippoorwill singing,
A blur in the darkness—my frilled dress of white.

Lost are those summertimes that I once knew—
Pump-squeak and shoe-squeak— faint melodies,
But always returning like echoes: the white dress
Still worn by a small girl in my memories.

—RUTH B. FIELD

MEMORY'S DOOR

Old homes, old towns, old friends,
Old ties we all hold dear,
All bind us closer to the past
With every passing year.
The far horizons lure
And beckon us; in youth
We journey forth for fortune, fame,
Or maybe search for truth.

The hours, the days, the years
Speed blithely on their way
And all material things in life
So quickly fade away;

But memory holds the key
To joys we gladly share,
The hallowed scenes of childhood days
And loved ones dwelling there.

Old homes, old towns, old friends,
Old ties we all hold dear,
All locked within our memory
Grow dearer every year;
And when we use the key
That opens memory's door,
We see old homes, old towns, old friends
We loved long years before.

—DORA P. FORTNER

A Tribute to Grandmother

All that I can give to life will be
To hold a crimson sunset in the sky,
Or catch a birdsong as it flutters by,
Or string the stars on moonbeams that I see . . .
While all the things you have done for me —
And all the rest who often wonder why
You do so much and how your hands can fly —
Will be an unforgotten melody.

My poems and songs can only be the leaves . . .
Your life has been the tree.
— Mildred Maralyn Mercer

TITLE INDEX

FIRST LINE INDEX

AUTHOR INDEX

...understand the goodness of her...
...to know the warmth in a gra...
...lone, the good example she...
...ch she means from day to day...
...d things that children love.
...e for her keeps growing too,
...randmother's love has mean...
...ther love, how wise they a...